Contents

Moving

Things move in many ways.

Things can move fast or slowly.

Pushes

You can push things to make them move.

You can push things away from you.

You push a tyre to make it move.

8

You push a door to make it open.

You can push yourself up on
a see-saw.

You can push yourself along on
a scooter.

Heavy and light

Heavy things are hard to push.

A heavy wheelbarrow is hard to push.

Light things are easy to push.

A balloon is easy to push.

Big pushes

A big push can make heavy things move.

A big push can make things move faster.

Stopping

You can stop things with a push.

You can stop a ball with a push.

Moving things with a push

A push can move lots of different things.

What things do you move with a push?

What have you learned?

- A push can make something move.

- A push can make something stop moving.

- A big push can move heavy things.

- A big push can make things move faster.

ELIN	
Z752350	
PETERS	27-Feb-2012
531.11	£6.99

Picture glossary

push make something move away from you

Index

BETTWS

Notes for parents and teachers
Before reading
Explain to the children that one way of making things move is to push them. Demonstrate a few actions of pushing (e.g. pushing a door open, pushing a doll's pram, pushing a button on a toy). Ask the children if it is easy to push a heavy thing or a light thing? Show the children how you can move a toy car across the floor with one push.

After reading
• Give four children each a toy car. They should start from a starting point. They each have one push. Whose car goes the furthest?
• Stand the children in a circle facing inwards with their palms touching the palms of the children on either side. Choose one child to start to give a gentle push in one direction. Can they pass the push around the circle?
• Sit in a circle in the hall. Give each child a number. Give one child a bean bag. Call out a number and the child must push the bean bag across to that child. Then call out another number and that child pushes the bean bag on.